SAY WHAT I AM:

A BOOK OF OLD ENGLISH RIDDLES

SAY WHAT I AM:
A BOOK OF OLD ENGLISH RIDDLES

translated by Ben Waggoner

© 2017
The Troth

© 2017, The Troth, Inc. All rights reserved. No part of this book may be reproduced or transmitted in any form or by any means, electronic or mechanical, including photocopy, recording, or any information storage and retrieval system, without prior permission in writing from the publisher. Exceptions may be allowed for non-commercial "fair use," for the purposes of news reporting, criticism, comment, scholarship, research, or teaching.

Second Edition

Earlier versions of many of these riddles have been published in *Idunna* magazine, 2008-2016.
An earlier edition of this collection was published in 2009 by Forsala Press.

Published by The Troth, Inc.
325 Chestnut Street, Suite 800
Philadelphia, Pennsylvania 19106
http://www.thetroth.org/

ISBN-13: 978-1-941136-11-9 (hardcover)
978-1-941136-10-2 (paperback)
978-1-941136-12-6 (e-book)

Cover image and image on pp. 31, 56: 12th-century ivory chess pieces from the Isle of Lewis, Scotland. Photos by Amanda Waggoner.

Cover design: Ben Waggoner

Troth logo designed by Kveldulf Gundarsson, drawn by 13 Labs, Chicago, Illinois

Typeset in Garamond 18/14/12/10

for my grandfather
Howell Holmes Gwin

Sum bið boca gleaw,
larum leoþufæst.   Sum biþ listhendig
to awritanne   wordgeryno. . . .
Swa weorðlice   wide tosaweð
Dryhten his duguþe.

A single manuscript, the Exeter Book, is the largest surviving collection of poetry in Old English. Among many other poems, it includes a collection of riddles: one in Latin, and the rest in alliterative Old English verse. The book may have once contained one hundred riddles. In the standard modern edition, ninety-five are present now. However, about ten of the riddles are fragmentary, either because of damage to the manuscript or because the copyist accidentally omitted too much of a riddle to make its meaning clear. Other riddles may or may not be composites of separate texts. Thus there is some uncertainty as to just how many riddles there are.

The Exeter Book itself is known to have existed before 1072, when Bishop Leofric died. He is known to have donated books to Exeter Cathedral, including *mycel englisc boc be gehwilcum þingum on leoðwisan geworht*—"a large book in English, about various things, composed in poetry", almost certainly the Exeter Book itself.[1] The book may have been copied decades earlier, by a single scribe—all of the text is in a single hand. The riddles may have been composed earlier still, but the date of their composition is still uncertain.[2]

The book in your hands contains a selection of forty-nine of these riddles. These have been chosen solely according to the translator's tastes, but provide a representative sample of the Exeter Book riddles. I've chosen to add two additional riddles from a somewhat obscure Old English poem called *Solomon and Saturn*. Saturn, the Roman god of agriculture who presided over a golden age, embodies pagan wisdom; he is depicted asking questions of Solomon, the Biblical king who represents Judeo-Christian wisdom. At two points in the poem, Saturn proposes a riddle that Solomon quickly solves.

History of Old English Riddles

Although riddles are known from oral tradition in a great many cultures, the tradition of literary riddles in England seems to owe its existence to late Latin literature. A collection of one hundred Latin riddles (*Aenigmata*) by Symphosius, probably dating from the late 4th or early 5th century CE, was popular in the early Middle Ages. Three of the Exeter Book riddles (47, 85, and 86) are translated or adapted from Symphosius's riddles, and others make use of images and phrases found in his work.

Symphosius's *Aenigmata* inspired Anglo-Saxon monks to write their own riddles in Latin. While the riddles of Symphosius are each three lines long and give the solution in the title, Anglo-Saxon Latin riddles are more varied in length and form. The best-known English author of Latin riddles is Aldhelm, Abbot of Malmesbury and later Bishop of Sherborne (639–705). Two of the Exeter Book riddles (35 and 40) are translations of riddles by Aldhelm. Other English composers of Latin riddles include Tatwine, Eusebius, and Boniface, although their riddles seem to have no direct effect on the Exeter Book riddles.

The composers of Old English riddles may have been inspired by the learned Latin riddle tradition, but they certainly made it their own; as noted above, relatively few can be called translations of Latin riddles. Where some of Aldhelm's riddles deal with exotic subjects—gemstones, stars, strange beasts, mythological monsters—the Old English riddles are more likely to deal with everyday subjects: household and farm tools, weapons, familiar animals and birds. Even when they do treat the same subject as one of Aldhelm's riddles, they often take a different approach to describing their subject. And unlike Symphosius's riddles, they do not give the answer in the title, or anywhere. Scholars since the late 19th century have proposed solutions, and while many of the riddles are generally agreed to have been solved, some remain contentious.

Riddles in Old English Literature

The Exeter Book riddles are perhaps not the summit of poetry in Old English, but they possess a charm all their own. Formally, they are fairly standard examples of alliterative verse, but some diaplay additional tricks of the poet's trade, such as end-rhymes (most notably in Riddle 28), the use of runes to encode answers and clues, and various puns and other wordplay. As for the riddles' content, not only do they paint vivid scenes, they give a voice to personages that aren't often heard from in Old English poetry. For example, the ideal of heroism unto death is nowhere better expressed than in *The Battle of Maldon*:

Hige sceal þe heardra,   heorte þe cenre,
mod sceal þe mare,   þe ure mægen lytlað.
Her lið ure ealdor   eall forheawen,
god on greote.   A mæg gnornian
se ðe nu fram þis wigplegan   wendan þenceð.
Ic eom frod feores;   fram ic ne wille,
ac ic me be healfe   minum hlaforde,
be swa leofan men,   licgan þence.

Mind must he harder,   heart be keener,
courage be more   as our might weakens.
There lies our lord   struck down completely,
a good man, on the gravel.   May he grieve forever
who thinks to flee   from this battle-play.
I am aged in life;   I don't wish to leave,
but by the side   of my lord,
by such a beloved man,   I think to lie.

But an opposing voice appears in Riddle 5. This riddle is spoken by a shield, but it sounds like the speech of any war-weary soldier who just wants to get out of the battle alive and go home—and who knows that this isn't likely. Like Byrhtwold in *The Battle of Maldon*, the shield sees the hopelessness of the situation. Unlike Byrhtwold, the shield has no hope of winning eternal glory:

Ic eom anhaga   iserne wund,
bille gebennad,   beadoweorca sæd,
ecgum werig.   Oft ic wig seo,
frecne feohtan.   Frofre ne wene,
þæt me geoc cyme   guðgewinnes,
ær ic mid ældum   eal forwurðe...

I am all alone,   iron-wounded,
slashed by swords,   sated with battle's work,
weary of weapons.   War I see often,
fiercest fighting.   I can't feign hope
that relief might reach me   in the rage of battle
before I perish   completely in flames...

Plenty of passages in *Beowulf* deal with the warrior's joys in the mead-hall, drinking ale and mead, listening to the scop's harp-song, and receiving golden gifts from one's lord and king. Sex isn't mentioned as a mead-hall enjoyment. And yet Riddle 54, which is clearly intended to make the listener think naughty thoughts, hints that rather more carnal instincts could be gratified in the hall:

> *Hyse cwom gangan. . . .*
> *hof his agen*
> *hrægl hondum up,   hrand under gyrdels*
> *hyre stondendre   stiþes nathwæt. . . .*

> So this guy walks in. . . .
> hiked his own clothes
> up with his hands,   and under her girdle
> he stuck a stiff thingie,   as she was standing right there.

The author or compiler of these riddles was even able to write himself into the collection. In Riddle 51, whose answer is "fingers and quill pen writing", the author is the "warrior" who leads the fingers and pen onward:

> *Dreag unstille*
> *winnende wiga   se him wegas tæcneþ*
> *ofer fæted gold   feower eallum.*

> A doughty warrior
> persevered in pointing out   the path to all four,
> so that they might ride   over richest gold.

We get detailed descriptions of the less heroic side of Anglo-Saxon life—the ploughs, rakes, ovens, butter churns, and other unglamorous tools—alongside the armor and weapons and drinking horns and strong drink of warriors and kings. Women's voices appear in the Exeter Book riddles. So do women's traditional tasks in Anglo-Saxon society—baking, weaving, churning butter, caring for their menfolk—while the "Iceberg" riddle hints at a darker, grimmer side to femininity, perhaps drawn from the same depths as Grendel's mother in *Beowulf* or the troll-wives and witches of folklore. The natural world also appears: birds, animals, bees, storms, and even the entirety of nature—possibly even death itself—are allowed to speak for themselves through these riddles.

Two of the most common words in these riddles are *wundor*, "wonder; marvel", and *wrætlic*, which can mean "splendid, beautiful, excellent" or "wondrous, strange, curious." With their puzzling metaphorical language, these riddles direct our attention to the *wundor* that hides in plain sight. Even the humblest of household tools or most familiar of animals may turn out to be *wrætlic*—both curious and strange, and at the same time, excellent and beautiful. In the world of the riddles, everyday existence is revealed as something unexpectedly rich, lovely, humorous, and awe-inspiring. I hope that my translations have managed to bring out something of this.

The original Old English texts are taken from Krapp and Dobie's *Anglo-Saxon Poetic Records*; I have followed the numbering used in this work, and generally followed the emendations and textual notes given in this work, except where noted. I've tried to follow the alliterative scheme of Old English poetry, albeit occasionally relaxing the rules when there seemed no readable alternative. When possible, I have tried to convey the stylistic quirks of certain riddles (such as the rhymes in Riddles 2 and 28, or the pun in Riddle 35), without making the syntax or vocabulary too obscure and high-flown. Some of my previously published translations have been lightly revised for this edition.

I thank Énbarr Coleman and Amanda Waggoner for their helpful comments and critiques.

Riddle 1

Hwylc is hælepa þæs horsc ond þæs hygecræftig
þæt þæt mæge asecgan, hwa mec on sið wræce,
þonne ic astige strong, stundum reþe,
þrymful þunie, þragum wræce
fere geond foldan, folcsalo bærne,
ræced reafige? Recas stigað,
haswe ofer hrofum. Hlin bið on eorþan,
wælcwealm wera, þonne ic wudu hrere,
bearwas bledhwate, beamas fylle,
holme gehrefed, heahum meahtum
wrecen on waþe, wide sended;
hæbbe me on hrycge þæt ær hadas wreah
foldbuendra, flæsc ond gæstas,
somod on sunde. Saga hwa mec þecce,
oþþe hu ic hatte, þe þa hlæst bere.

    What comrade's so canny, so crafty in mind
    that he dares name the one who drives me on course
    when I mount up, mighty, maddened sometimes,
    with terrible tumult? At times, ruin's what
    I bear through the land: I burn the folk's hall,
    smash the palace down. Smoke, hoar-grey,
    rises over roofs. There are rumblings on earth,
    warriors are whelmed; as I whip through stands
    of flourishing trees, I fell their trunks.
    Covered by water I wander, driven
    by mighty powers, dispatched far and wide.
    I carry on my back what once covered those
    abiding on land, their bodies and souls
    together in the streams. Say who covers me,
    or how I, the bearer of this burden, am called.

Riddle 2

*Hwilum ic gewite, swa ne wenaþ men,
under ypa geþræc eorþan secan,
garsecges grund. Gifen biþ gewreged,
fam gewealcen. . . .
hwælmere hlimmeð, hlude grimmeð,
streamas staþu beatað, stundum weorpaþ
on stealc hleoþa stane ond sonde,
ware ond wæge, þonne ic winnende,
holmmægne biþeaht, hrusan styrge,
side sægrundas. Sundhelme ne mæg
losian ær mec læte se þe min latteow bið
on siþa gehwam. Saga, þoncol mon,
hwa mec bregde of brimes fæþmum,
þonne streamas eft stille weorþað,
yþa geþwære, þe mec ær wrugon.*

    Sometimes I set out   unseen by men
    under a mob of waves   to maul the earth,
    the Spear-Wielder's land.   The sea is wakened,
    spume set swirling. . . .
    the whale-mere lashes,   loudly smashes,
    currents crash into   the coast, at times tossing
    stones and sand,   seaweed and waves,
    up the steep banks   as I battle in secret,
    concealed by sea-might,   stirring up the bottom,
    the billows' wide bed.   But I can never
    hide myself under   the helm of the depths
    unless *he* allows it—   my leader and guide
    on all my travels.   Tell me, thoughtful man,
    who brings me up   from the brine's clutches
    when ocean's currents   are calmed again,
    when waves are serene   that once hid me.

Riddle 5

Ic eom anhaga iserne wund,
bille gebennad, beadoweorca sæd,
ecgum werig. Oft ic wig seo,
frecne feohtan. Frofre ne wene,
þæt me geoc cyme guðgewinnes,
ær ic mid ældum eal forwurðe,
ac mec hnossiað homera lafe,
heardecg heoroscearp, hondweorc smiþa,
bitað in burgum; ic abidan sceal
laþran gemotes. Næfre læcecynn
on folcstede findan meahte,
þara þe mid wyrtum wunde gehælde,
ac me ecga dolg eacen weorðað
þurh deaðslege dagum ond nihtum.

  I am all alone, iron-wounded,
  slashed by swords, sated with battle's work,
  weary of weapons. War I see often,
  fiercest fighting. I can't feign hope
  that relief might reach me in the rage of battle
  before I perish completely in flames,
  but I am hurt by hammer-leavings:
  the hard edge, honed for war, handwork of smiths,
  bites within the walls; I must withstand
  even crueler encounters. No kind of healer
  could I ever find in the folk-stead,
  who might have herbs to heal my wounds,
  but my blade-gashes grow ever larger
  from deadly blows, day and night.

Riddle 7

Hrægl min swigað,   þonne ic hrusan trede,
oþþe þa wic buge,   oþþe wado drefe.
Hwilum mec ahebbað   ofer hæleþa byht
hyrste mine,   ond þeos hea lyft,
ond mec þonne wide   wolcna strengu
ofer folc byreð.   Frætwe mine
swogað hlude   ond swinsiað,
torhte singað,   þonne ic getenge ne beom
flode ond foldan,   ferende gæst.

    My clothes make no clatter   when I creep on the earth,
    when I stay in my home   or stir up the waters.
    But my lovely dress   and the lofty air
    bear me up above   the abodes of men;
    sky-strength sends me   soaring high over
    the folk, faring far.   My fine apparel
    makes a melody,   moaning aloud,
    singing sweetly   as I sail, a wanderer
    not weighted down   by water and land.

Riddle 8

Ic þurh muþ sprece mongum reordum,
wrencum singe, wrixle geneahhe
heafodwoþe, hlude cirme,
healde mine wisan, hleoþre ne miþe,
eald æfensceop, eorlum bringe
blisse in burgum, þonne ic bugendre
stefne styrme; stille on wicum
sittað nigende. Saga hwæt ic hatte,
þe swa scirenige sceawendwisan
hlude onhyrge, hæleþum bodige
wilcumena fela woþe minre.

  I speak through my mouth with many voices;
  I sing with a flourish, frequently change
  my high caroling, cry out aloud,
  stay with my old ways and don't stint my song.
  Twilight's old bard, I bring such joy
  to townsfolk, when I take my bow
  and let loose my music; they listen, reverent,
  hushed in their homes. How am I called,
  who brazenly mimics the minstrel's lays
  like a clever comic, proclaiming to men
  many welcome tidings with my warbling voice?

Riddle 11

Hrægl is min hasofag,   hyrste beorhte,
reade ond scire   on reafe minum.
Ic dysge dwelle   ond dole hwette
unrædsiþas,   oþrum styre
nyttre fore.   Ic þæs nowiht wat
þæt heo swa gemædde,   mode bestolene,
dæde gedwolene,   deoraþ mine
won wisan gehwam.   Wa him þæs þeawes,
siþþan heah bringað   horda deorast,
gif hi unrædes   ær ne geswicaþ.

    Grey is my garb,   gleaming with jewels,
    radiant red   on the robes I wear.
    I dupe dolts,   and to dullards I suggest
    stupid schemes;   I steer others away
    from decent endeavors.   I don't know how
    they can be such morons,   with their minds stolen,
    their deeds so depraved,   that they'd praise my habits,
    my wickedness, to anyone.   Woe to them all
    who hold up on high   this hoard, so costly,
    if they don't first forsake   their foolishness.

Riddle 13

Ic seah turf tredan,   X wæron ealra,
VI gebroþor   ond hyra sweostor mid;
hæfdon feorg cwico.   Fell hongedon
sweotol ond gesyne   on seles wæge
anra gehwylces.   Ne wæs hyra ængum þy wyrs,
ne siðe þy sarre,   þeah hy swa sceoldon
reafe birofene,   rodra weardes
meahtum aweahte,   muþum slitan
haswe blede.   Hrægl bið geniwad
þam þe ær forðcymene   frætwe leton
licgan on laste,   gewitan lond tredan.

    I saw six brothers,   their sisters also:
ten in all   were treading the earth,
ten living souls.   A skin garment
hung on the wall   in the home of each,
plain to be seen.   None suffered pain,
none had a hard lot,   although Heaven's Warder
hed robbed them of raiment,   roused them all
by his sacred strength   to snap with their mouths
at gray-green shoots.   There's new garb for them
who first came forth,   their finery stripped,
to stand on their feet   and stride on the ground.

Riddle 14

Ic wæs wæpenwiga.   Nu mec wlonc þeceð
geong hagostealdmon   golde ond sylfore,
woum wirbogum.   Hwilum weras cyssað,
hwilum ic to hilde   hleoþre bonne
wilgehleþan,   hwilum wycg byreþ
mec ofer mearce,   hwilum merehengest
fereð ofer flodas   frætwum beorhtne,
hwilum mægða sum   minne gefylleð
bosm beaghroden;   hwilum ic bordum sceal,
heard, heafodleas,   behlyþed licgan,
hwilum hongige   hyrstum frætwed,
wlitig on wage,   þær weras drincað,
freolic fyrdsceorp.   Hwilum folcwigan
on wicge wegað,   þonne ic winde sceal
sincfag swelgan   of sumes bosme;
hwilum ic gereordum   rincas laðige
wlonce to wine;   hwilum wraþum sceal
stefne minre   forstolen hreddan,
flyman feondsceaþan.   Frige hwæt ic hatte.

I was a war-weapon.   Now I'm wound all about
by a stalwart young thane   with silver and gold,
wrought with wire-work.   Warriors may kiss me;
sometimes my song   summons jolly companions
to brace for battle.   Or I'm borne by a horse
across border-marches,   or the brine-stallion
ferries me over floods,   finely bejeweled.
Sometimes a lady,   lovely in her rings,
fills up my belly.   On boards, at times,
deprived of my head—   a hard lot!—I must lie.
Sometimes, beautiful   and brave in my finery,
I hang on the wall   where heroes drink,
fair fighting-gear.   Or else folk-warriors
bear me on horseback   when, bright with treasure,
I must swallow the breath   out of someone's bosom.
Sometimes my voice   invites proud men
to partake of wine;   or my tongue must scream
to free the goods   that foes have stolen,
routing enemies.   Ask what I'm called.

Riddle 16

Oft ic sceal wiþ wæge winnan   ond wiþ winde feohtan,
somod wið þam sæcce,   þonne ic secan gewite
eorþan yþum þeaht;   me biþ se eþel fremde.
Ic beom strong þæs gewinnes,   gif ic stille weorþe;
gif me þæs tosæleð,   hi beoð swiþran þonne ic,
ond mec slitende   sona flymað,
willað oþfergan   þæt ic friþian sceal.
Ic him þæt forstonde,   gif min steort þolað
ond mec stiþne wiþ   stanas moton
fæste gehabban.   Frige hwæt ic hatte.

I must often struggle against waves   and strive against winds,
fight them together,   when I fare forth to seek
the wave-thatched earth;   land's alien to me.
If I can stand quite still,   I'm strong in that battle;
if matters go amiss,   they'll prove mightier than I,
and they'll put me to rout,   ripping me away.
They mean to make off   with what I must defend.
I'll protect it, as long as   my tail holds out
and the stones can seize me,   the stout one—keep me
guarded in their grasp.   Guess what I'm called.

Riddle 17

Ic eom mundbora   minre heorde,
eodorwirum fæst,   innan gefylled
dryhtgestreona.   Dægtidum oft
spæte sperebrogan;   sped biþ þy mare
fylle minre.   Frea þæt bihealdeð,
hu me of hrife fleogað   hyldepilas.
Hwilum ic sweartum   swelgan onginne
brunum beadowæpnum,   bitrum ordum,
eglum attorsperum.   Is min innað til,
wombhord wlitig,   wloncum deore;
men gemunan   þæt me þurh muþ fareð.

I give safe harbor   to my herds and flocks,
bound up with bands   to bear within me
my folk's dear treasure.   By day I often
spit spear-terror;   success is greater
the more I am filled.   My master beholds
how fighting darts fly   forth from my midriff.
Sometimes I start   to swallow whole
the black-brown battle-weapons,   bitter-sharp points,
evil venom-spears.   But my innards are good,
a beautiful belly-hoard;   brave men prize it—
though they must mind   what my mouth gives out.

Riddle 19

Ic on siþe seah . ᛋ ᚱ ᚠ
ᚾ . *hygewloncne,   heafodbeorhtne,*
swiftne ofer sælwong   swiþe þrægan.
Hæfde him on hrycge   hildeþryþe
. ᛏ ᚠ ᛗ .   *nægledne rad*
. ᚠ ᚷ ᛗ ᚹ .   *Widlast ferede*
rynestrong on rade   rofne . ᚳ ᚠ
ᚹ ᚠ ᚠ ᚾ .   *For wæs þy beorhtre,*
swylcra siþfæt.   Saga hwæt ic hatte.

      I saw sally forth   **Equine Sun's Ride, Oaken Hail**, high-hearted,   its head bright,
      over fair fields   a fast courser.
      It bore on its back   battle strength;
      Need's Ash-Man   on the nailed one, riding
      Sun's Yew, Ash-Wonder.   On his wide travels
      the strong rider bore   a bold, **Keen Wonder**
      of **Ash** and **Hail**.   Such heroes' riding out
      was so much the brighter.   Say what I'm called.

Riddle 21

*Neb is min niþerweard; neol ic fere
ond be grunde græfe, geonge swa me wisað
har holtes feond, ond hlaford min
woh færeð weard æt steorte,
wrigaþ on wonge, wegeð mec ond þyð,
saweþ on swæð min. Ic snyþige forð,
brungen of bearwe, bunden cræfte,
wegen on wægne, hæbbe wundra fela;
me biþ gongendre grene on healfe
ond min swæð sweotol sweart on oþre.
Me þurh hrycg wrecen hongaþ under
an orþoncpil, oþer on heafde,
fæst ond forðweard. Fealleþ on sidan
þæt ic toþum tere, gif me teala þenaþ
hindeweardre, þæt biþ hlaford min.*

    My beak bends downwards; on my belly I creep
as I grub in the ground. I go down the path
that the grey-haired foe of the forest shows me.
The warden of my tail end walks bent over,
passing through the field he pushes and shoves me
and sows in my wake. I sniff along the ground,
when I'm carried from the copse, carefully tied up,
wheeled on a wagon. Many wonders I hold:
the groove where I've gone is green on one side,
my broad byway is black on the other.
A spike made with skill has been stuck through my back
and hangs down beneath; there's another on my head,
fixed firmly in front. What my fangs tear up
slips to the side, if my sovereign lord
properly serves me as he presses from behind.

Riddle 22

Ætsomne cwom   LX monna
to wægstæpe   wicgum ridan;
hæfdon XI   eoredmæcgas
fridhengestas,   IIII sceamas.
Ne meahton magorincas   ofer mere feolan,
swa hi fundedon,   ac wæs flod to deop,
atol yþa geþræc,   ofras hea,
streamas stronge.   Ongunnon stigan þa
on wægn weras   ond hyra wicg somod
hlodan under hrunge;   þa þa hors oðbær
eh ond eorlas,   æscum dealle,
ofer wætres byht   wægn to lande,
swa hine oxa ne teah   ne esna mægen
ne fæthengest,   ne on flode swom,
ne be grunde wod   gestum under,
ne lagu drefde,   ne on lyfte fleag,
ne under bæc cyrde;   brohte hwæþre
beornas ofer burnan   ond hyra bloncan mid
from stæðe heaum,   þæt hy stopan up
on operne,   ellenrofe
weras of wæge,   ond hyra wicg gesund.

Sixty men, all   mounted on horses
assembled together   on the sea's rim;
this troop of horsemen   had eleven
of the finest palfreys,   and four bright steeds.
The strapping lads couldn't   cross the sea
as they wished to do,   for the water was too deep,
the billows were breaking,   the banks were high,
the flows too strong.   So the fellows began
to step up on a wagon,   and their steeds all together
they held beneath the pole.   Then a horse pulled
the earls, splendid   with their spears, and their horses,
across the bay waters,   bringing them to land.
Oxen did not pull it,   nor the power of slaves,
nor any dray-horse;   it neither drifted on the sea,
nor paced on dry land   with passengers on top,
nor roiled the water,   nor rose into the air,
nor stopped to turn back.   Yet still, it carried
the horses and riders   from one high bank
across the waters,   so that they came up
from the sea, stepping   safely on the far shore,
the bold-hearted men   and the mounts they rode.

Riddle 23

Agob is min noma eft onhwyrfed;
ic eom wrætlic wiht on gewin sceapen.
Þonne ic onbuge, ond me of bosme fareð
ætren onga, ic beom eallgearo
þæt ic me þæt feorhbealo feor aswape.
Siþþan me se waldend, se me þæt wite gescop,
leoþo forlæteð, ic beo lengre þonne ær,
oþþæt ic spæte, spilde geblonden,
ealfelo attor þæt ic ær geap.
Ne togongeð þæs gumena hwylcum,
ænigum eaþe þæt ic þær ymb sprice,
gif hine hrineð þæt me of hrife fleogeð,
þæt þone mandrinc mægne geceapaþ,
fullwered fæste feore sine.
Nelle ic unbunden ænigum hyran
nymþe searosæled. Saga hwæt ic hatte.

    "Wob" is my true name twisted around;
    I'm a wondrous wight: for war I was shaped.
    When I bend backwards, my bosom extends
    a poisonous sting; I prepare myself
    to fling that fatal bane far away from me.
    When my master, who made this misery for me,
    releases my limbs, I'm longer than I was,
    once I've spat out the strongest venom
    all blended with bale, which I bore before.
    There's no easy escape for any man,
    no getting away from this gall that I speak of,
    if he is touched by what tears from my belly:
    he pays with his power for that poisoned drink,
    buys the death-draught dearly—with his life.
    Unbound, I will never bow to anyone,
    unless I'm tied cunningly. Tell what I'm called.

Riddle 24

Ic eom wunderlicu wiht, wræsne mine stefne,
hwilum beorce swa hund, hwilum blæte swa gat,
hwilum græde swa gos, hwilum gielle swa hafoc,
hwilum ic onhyrge þone haswan earn,
guðfugles hleoþor, hwilum glidan reorde
muþe gemæne, hwilum mæwes song,
þær ic glado sitte. ᚷ mec nemnað,
swylce ᚫ ond ᚱ, ᚩ fullesteð,
ᚻ ond ᛁ . Nu ic haten eom
swa þa siex stafas sweotule becnaþ.

    I'm a wondrous wight, for I vary my voice:
    now I bark like a hound or bleat like a goat,
    now I honk like a goose or like a hawk I scream,
    and now I mimic the mist-grey eagle,
    the war-bird's cry. Now the kite's speech
    or the seagull's song I speak with my mouth
    where I sit proudly. A **Present** gives my name,
    also **Ash** and **God**; the **Elm** completes it
    with **Mist** and **Ice**. I have my name now:
    these six staves signify it plainly.

Riddle 27

Ic eom weorð werum,   wide funden,
brungen of bearwum   ond of burghleoþum,
of denum ond of dunum.   Dæges mec wægun
feþre on lifte,   feredon mid liste
under hrofes hleo.   Hæleð mec siþþan
baþedan in bydene.   Nu ic eom bindere
ond swingere,   sona weorþe
esne to eorþan,   hwilum ealdne ceorl.
Sona þæt onfindeð,   se þe mec fehð ongean,
ond wið mægenþisan   minre genæsteð,
þæt he hrycge sceal   hrusan secan,
gif he unrædes   ær ne geswiceð,
strengo bistolen,   strong on spræce,
mægene binumen;   nah his modes geweald,
fota ne folma.   Frige hwæt ic hatte,
ðe on eorþan swa   esnas binde,
dole æfter dyntum   be dæges leohte.

I'm favored by folk   and found far and wide,
gathered from groves   and from garths on heights,
from dales and downs.   Each day, many wings
fly me through the air,   ferry me with skill
to a high-roofed haven.   A hero then takes me
and bathes me in a barrel.   Now I'm a binder
and a flogger of fools;   soon I fling down
a servant to earth,   or sometimes an old churl.
He who would fight me   finds out soon,
when he struggles against   my strength and power,
that his back will hit   the hardened earth
if he doesn't forsake   the silly notion first;
his strength is stolen.   He's strong in speech,
but his might is taken,   his mind-strength fails
his feet and hands.   Figure out what I'm called,
who on earth binds   bondsmen this way,
deals blows to blockheads   in broad daylight.

Riddle 28

Biþ foldan dæl   fægre gegierwed
mid þy heardestan   ond mid þy scearpestan
ond mid þy grymmestan   gumena gestreona,
corfen, sworfen,   cyrred, þyrred,
bunden, wunden,   blæced, wæced,
frætwed, geatwed,   feorran læded
to durum dryhta.   Dream bið in innan
cwicra wihta,   clengeð, lengeð,
þara þe ær lifgende   longe hwile
wilna bruceð   ond no wið spriceð,
ond þonne æfter deaþe   deman onginneð,
meldan mislice.   Micel is to hycganne
wisfæstum menn,   hwæt seo wiht sy.

    A field on the earth   is finely bedecked
    with the hardest   and with the sharpest
    and with the cruelest   crop that men grow:
    reaped and heaped,   raked and baked,
    bundled and trundled,   bleached and leached,
    dressed in its best,   and brought from afar
    to people's homes.   Happiness enters
    all living beings,   lasting long, bringing song;
    those who have lived   for a long time
    relish this pleasure   and won't rail against it.
    Even after death   they deem and debate
    in several ways.   To solve this is hard
    for the wisest of wits: what wight is this?

Riddle 29

*Ic wiht geseah   wundorlice
hornum bitweonum   huþe lædan,
lyftfæt leohtlic,   listum gegierwed,
huþe to þam ham   of þam heresiþe;
walde hyre on þære byrig   bur atimbran,
searwum asettan,   gif hit swa meahte.
ða cwom wundorlicu wiht   ofer wealles hrof,
seo is eallum cuð   eorðbuendum,
ahredde þa þa huþe   ond to ham bedraf
wreccan ofer willan,   gewat hyre west þonan
fæhþum feran,   forð onette.
Dust stonc to heofonum,   deaw feol on eorþan,
niht forð gewat.   Nænig siþþan
wera gewiste   þære wihte sið.*

    Once I witnessed   a wondrous creature
    bear plundered treasure   between his horns:
    a cup, held aloft,   well-crafted and shining.
    He fetched home his prize   from the field of battle,
    wishing to build   a bower in his fortress,
    crafted with cunning,   if he could construct it.
    Then a wondrous creature   came over the wall;
    she's known to all beings   who abide on the earth.
    She retook the plunder   and compelled the outlaw
    to hurry for home.   He headed west
    on a hasty voyage,   with vengeance in mind.
    Dust rose to heaven,   dew fell to earth,
    night passed away.   No man afterwards
    knew where that wight   had wandered to.

Riddle 31

Is þes middangeard   missenlicum
wisum gewlitegad,   wrættum gefrætwad.
Ic seah sellic þing   singan on ræcede;
wiht wæs nower   werum on gemonge,
sio hæfde wæstum   wundorlicran.
Niþerweard   wæs neb hyre,
fet ond folme   fugele gelice;
no hwæþre fleogan mæg   ne fela gongan,
hwæþre feþegeorn   fremman onginneð,
gecoren cræftum,   cyrreð geneahhe
oft ond gelome   eorlum on gemonge,
siteð æt symble,   sæles bideþ,
hwonne ær heo cræft hyre   cyþan mote
werum on wonge.   Ne heo þær wiht þigeð
þæs þe him æt blisse   beornas habbað.
Deor domes georn,   hio dumb wunað;
hwæþre hyre is on fote   fæger hleoþor,
wynlicu woðgiefu.   Wrætlic me þinceð,
hu seo wiht mæge   wordum lacan
þurh fot neoþan,   frætwed hyrstum.
Hafað hyre on halse,   þonne hio hord warað,
bær, beagum deall,   broþor sine,
mæg mid mægne.   Micel is to hycgenne
wisum woðboran,   hwæt sio wiht sie.

This Middle-Earth   in so many ways
is made fair and fine,   furnished with wonders.
I saw a strange thing   singing in the hall;
never was this being   numbered among men,
her features and form   more fanciful still.
Her nose is turned   to hang netherwards,
her feet and hands   have the form of a bird's,
though she cannot fly   nor fare anywhere.
Would that she could walk!   She's willing to show off
her excellent art.   Often enough
she roams around   through the ranks of earls,
waits at the feast   for the fixed time
when she may proclaim   her precious skill
to men in the field.   Not a mite does she share
of what gives heroes   happiness and joy.
The beast loves praise   but she lacks speech,
yet in her foot   a fair voice she has,
a glorious song-gift—   a great wonder
how this creature   can craft word-lays
through her down-dangling,   decorated foot.
Graced with rings,   when she guards her hoard,
she bears her brothers   on her bare neck—
what a mighty maiden!   Musing on this riddle
is no simple task   for sage counselors.

Riddle 32

Is þes middangeard   missenlicum
wisum gewlitegad,   wrættum gefrætwad.
Siþum sellic   ic seah searo hweorfan,
grindan wið greote,   giellende faran.
Næfde sellicu wiht   syne ne folme,
exle ne earmas;   sceal on anum fet
searoceap swifan,   swiþe feran,
faran ofer feldas.   Hæfde fela ribba;
muð wæs on middan.   Moncynne nyt,
fereð foddurwelan,   folcscipe dreogeð,
wist in wigeð,   ond werum gieldeð
gaful geara gehwam   þæs þe guman brucað,
rice ond heane.   Rece, gif þu cunne,
wis worda gleaw,   hwæt sio wiht sie.

    This Middle-Earth   in so many ways
    is made fair and fine,   furnished with wonders.
    I once saw a marvel   moving with skill,
    grinding on gravel,   groaning as it went.
    The strange thing had   no sight, no hands,
    shoulders nor arms;   this odd contraption
    must swiftly sweep past   while standing on one foot
    as it roams the fields.   Ribs it has in plenty
    and a mouth in its middle.   For mankind's needs,
    it brings abundance,   busily laboring,
    carrying supplies   and completely yielding
    all manner of tribute   that men most enjoy,
    whether rich or poor.   Reckon if you can,
    wise man with words,   what this wight might be.

Riddle 33

Wiht cwom æfter wege   wrætlicu liþan,
cymlic from ceole   cleopode to londe,
hlinsade hlude;   hleahtor wæs gryrelic,
egesful on earde,   ecge wæron scearpe.
Wæs hio hetegrim,   hilde to sæne,
biter beadoweorca;   bordweallas grof,
heardhiþende.   Heterune bond,
sægde searocræftig   ymb hyre sylfre gesceaft:
"Is min modor   mægða cynnes
þæs deorestan,   þæt is dohtor min
eacen up liden,   swa þæt is ældum cuþ,
firum on folce,   þæt seo on foldan sceal
on ealra londa gehwam   lissum stondan."

    A wight o'er the wave   came wondrously sailing.
    From ship to shore   she shouted out boldly,
    loudly resounding;   her laughter was terrifying,
    horrible on land;   well-honed, her blades.
    She was savage with hatred,   slow to the fight
    but bitter in battle-work,   bashing wood walls,
    harrowing harshly.   Hate-runes she bound.
    The treacherous one   told of her own nature:
    "Of all maidens,   my mother is the one
    most dearly loved;   my daughter is she,
    raised up on high.   Humankind knows,
    each of the folk,   that in every land
    she shall stand on the ground   granting mercies to all."

Riddle 34

Ic wiht geseah in wera burgum,
seo þæt feoh fedeð. Hafað fela toþa;
nebb biþ hyre æt nytte, niþerweard gongeð,
hiþeð holdlice ond to ham tyhð,
wæþeð geond weallas, wyrte seceð;
aa heo þa findeð, þa þe fæst ne biþ;
læteð hio þa wlitigan, wyrtum fæste,
stille stondan on staþolwonge,
beorhte blican, blowan ond growan.

    I saw a strange creature in the settlements of men,
    a tender of cattle— many teeth in her mouth.
    Her beak benefits her; it is bent downwards.
    She faithfully pillages, then fares back homewards;
    past the walls, she plunders the plants that she seeks.
    She always finds those not firmly rooted,
    but allows the lovely, long-growing plants
    to stand at their ease in established fields,
    brightly shining, blooming and growing.

Riddle 35

Mec se wæta wong,   wundrum freorig,
of his innaþe   ærist cende.
Ne wat ic mec beworhtne   wulle flysum,
hærum þurh heahcræft,   hygeþoncum min.
Wundene me ne beoð wefle,   ne ic wearp hafu,
ne þurh þreata geþræcu   þræd me ne hlimmeð,
ne æt me hrutende   hrisil scriþeð,
ne mec ohwonan   sceal am cnyssan.
Wyrmas mec ne awæfan   wyrda cræftum,
þa þe geolo godwebb   geatwum frætwað.
Wile mec mon hwæþre seþeah   wide ofer eorþan
hatan for hæleþum   hyhtlic gewæde.
Saga soðcwidum,   searoþoncum gleaw,
wordum wisfæst,   hwæt þis gewæde sy.

    The boggy meadow,   bitterly cold,
first birthed me forth   from its frigid womb.
I know in my heart   that I never was fashioned
by fine finger-work   from fleece or from hair.
I have no twisted weft,   no warp either:
not for me the thrumming   of threads pressed and taut,
nor the whirring shuttle   that whisks back and forth,
nor the weaving-slay   slashing me all over.
Worms did not weave me   with wise Norns' skill,
though they spin sumptuous   silk of gold.
Yet men near and far   nonetheless call me
a trusty garment   for tried heroes on earth.
If you're wise with words   and your wits are on guard,
then tell me truly   what this tunic might be.

Riddle 36

Ic wiht geseah   on wege feran,
seo wæs wrætlice   wundrum gegierwed.
Hæfde feowere   fet under wombe
ond ehtuwe   ufon on hrycge;
hæfde tu fiþru   ond twelf eagan
ond siex heafdu.   Saga hwæt hio wære.
For flodwegas;   ne wæs þæt na fugul ana,
ac þær wæs æghwylces   anra gelicnes
horses ond monnes,   hundes ond fugles,
ond eac wifes wlite.   Þu wast, gif þu const,
to gesecganne,   þæt we soð witan,
hu þære wihte   wise gonge.

     I saw some beast   start out on a journey,
     dearly adorned,   decked out with wonders.
     It had four feet   fitted below its belly,
     and eight more   were up on its back.
     It had twin wings   and twelve eyes
     and six heads in all.   Say what it was.
     It wended the waterways—   nor was it a bird only,
     but the likeness of each   was laid out to see:
     a horse and a man,   a hound and a bird,
     a woman's form also.   If you're able to say
     what we hold to be certain,   then soon you'll know
     how the nature of this beast   bears on its way.

Riddle 37

Ic þa wihte geseah; womb wæs on hindan
þriþum aþrunten. Þegn folgade,
mægenrofa man, ond micel hæfde
gefered þæt hit felde, fleah þurh his eage.
Ne swylteð he symle, þonne syllan sceal
innað þam oþrum, ac him eft cymeð
bot in bosme, blæd biþ aræred;
he sunu wyrceð, bið him sylfa fæder.

  I saw a beast whose belly was bulging behind him,
monstrously swollen. His servant followed him,
a brawny fellow. He bore a great load
of what filled him so full that it flew out of his eye.
Though he must give up his guts to others,
he does not die forever; often he receives
relief inside him, arising in glory.
He sires a son, himself his own father.

Riddle 38

Ic þa wiht geseah   wæpnedcynnes,
geoguðmyrþe grædig;   him on gafol forlet
ferðfriþende   feower wellan
scire sceotan,   on gesceap þeotan.
Mon maþelade,   se þe me gesægde:
"Seo wiht, gif hio gedygeð,   duna briceð;
gif he tobirsteð,   bindeð cwice."

    I saw a creature—the kind   that carries weapons,
    yearning for youths' joys.   He was yielded tribute:
    the giver of his life   granted him four springs
    bursting forth brightly,   bubbling up to please him.
    A man spoke up;   he said to me:
    "If that beast does well,   he breaks the hills.
    If he falls dead,   he fetters the living."

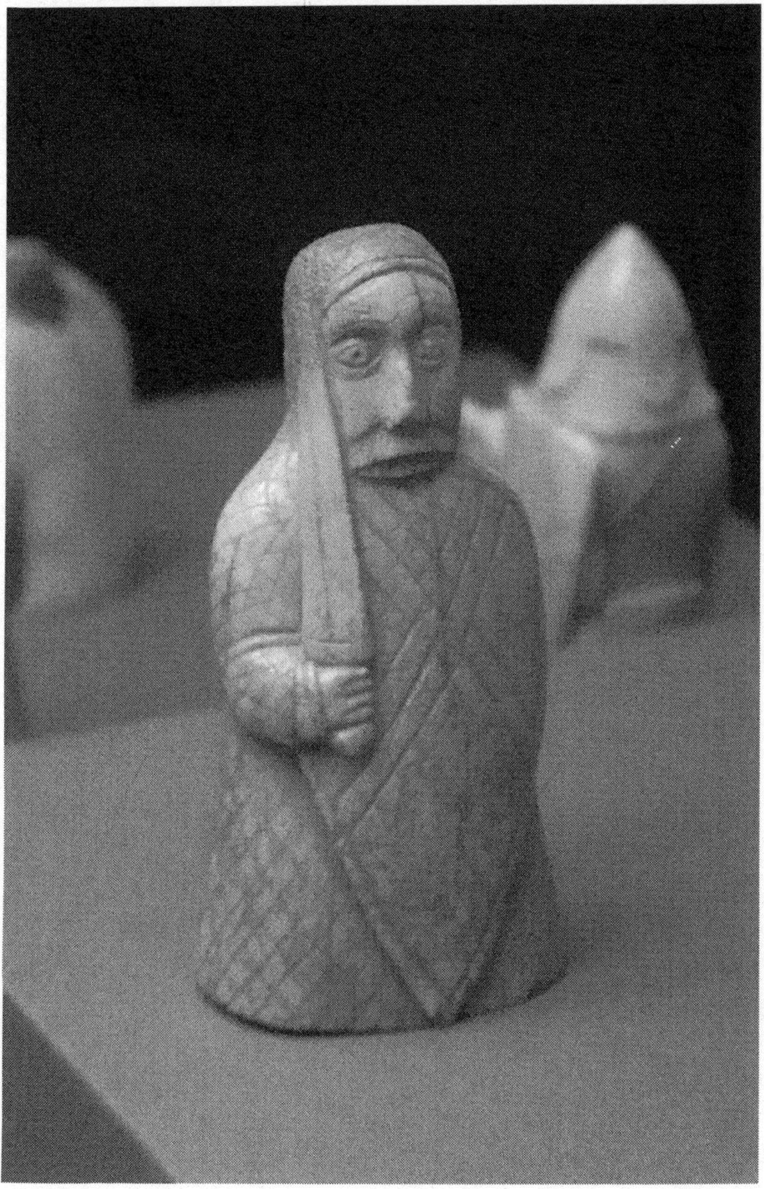

Riddle 39

Gewritu secgað   þæt seo wiht sy
mid moncynne   miclum tidum
sweotol ond gesyne.   Sundorcræft hafað
maran micle,   þonne hit men witen.
Heo wile gesecan   sundor æghwylcne
feorhberendra,   gewiteð eft feran on weg.
Ne bið hio næfre   niht þær oþre,
ac hio sceal wideferh   wreccan laste
hamleas hweorfan;   no þy heanre biþ.
Ne hafað hio fot ne folme,   ne æfre foldan hran,
ne eagena   ægþer twega,
ne muð hafaþ,   ne wiþ monnum spræc,
ne gewit hafað,   ac gewritu secgað
þæt seo sy earmost   ealra wihta,
þara þe æfter gecyndum   cenned wære.
Ne hafað hio sawle ne feorh,   ac hio siþas sceal
geond þas wundorworuld   wide dreogan.
Ne hafaþ hio blod ne ban,   hwæþre bearnum wearð
geond þisne middangeard   mongum to frofre.
Næfre hio heofonum hran,   ne to helle mot,
ac hio sceal wideferh   wuldorcyninges
larum lifgan.   Long is to secganne
hu hyre ealdorgesceaft   æfter gongeð,
woh wyrda gesceapu;   þæt is wrætlic þing
to gesecganne.   Soð is æghwylc
þara þe ymb þas wiht   wordum becneð;
ne hafað heo ænig lim,   leofaþ efne seþeah.
Gif þu mæge reselan   recene gesecgan
soþum wordum,   saga hwæt hio hatte.

Books bear witness   that this wight has been
plainly apparent   to people's sight
for countless ages.   She keeps her own power,
mightier by far   than men realize.
She will seek out   separate and alone
every living wight,   then leaves on her way,
never spending   a second night there;
she must wander   the way of exiles,
forever homeless,   but not humbled by it.
She has no feet or hands,   never feels the earth,
nor does she possess   a set of two eyes,
nor has she a mouth;   with men she speaks not,
nor has she reason.   Writings say
that she is lowliest   of all living wights
that were ever created   after their kind.
She has no soul or spirit;   she must suffer long journeys
through this world of wonders,   wandering far.
She has no blood or bones,   yet brings comfort
to many a man   throughout Middle-Earth.
She has never touched Heaven,   Hell is out of her reach,
but by the decrees   of the King of Glory
must she live forever.   Long is the telling
of how she is fated   to fare through her life
on wyrd's twisted ways—   a wondrous thing
that is to tell.   True are all things
concerning this wight   that words may reveal:
she has no limbs,   yet lives, even so.
If you can swiftly   speak the answer
in words of truth,   then tell her name.

Riddle 44

Wrætlic hongað   bi weres þeo,
frean under sceate.   Foran is þyrel.
Bið stiþ ond heard,   stede hafað godne;
þonne se esne   his agen hrægl
ofer cneo hefeð,   wile þæt cuþe hol
mid his hangellan   heafde gretan
þæt he efenlang ær   oft gefylde.

    A strange thing hangs   by the thigh of a man,
    under his tunic.   At the tip is a hole.
    It's stiff and hard,   standing quite firm.
    When the man hikes   the hem of his garment
    up over his knee,   he's eager to greet
    a familiar hole   with the head of his dangler—
    which he's frequently   filled up before.

Riddle 45

Ic on wincle gefrægn   weaxan nathwæt,
þindan ond þunian,   þecene hebban;
on þæt banlease   bryd grapode,
hygewlonc hondum,   hrægle þeahte
þrindende þing   þeodnes dohtor.

    Something in a corner   (so I heard) was growing,
    swelling and standing,   slipping off its covers.
    A bold-minded bride   gripped the boneless one
    with her own hands;   the high lord's daughter
    spread skirts over   the swollen thing.

Riddle 47

Moððe word fræt.   Me þæt þuhte
wrætlicu wyrd,   þa ic þæt wundor gefrægn,
þæt se wyrm forswealg   wera gied sumes,
þeof in þystro,   þrymfæstne cwide
ond þæs strangan staþol.   Stælgiest ne wæs
wihte þy gleawra,   þe he þam wordum swealg.

    A worm ate words.   A wonder it seemed,
    a curious fate,   when I caught wind of it:
    that this grub should gobble   glorious songs,
    this thief in the night   should nick fine speech,
    the proud man's support.   The pilfering guest
    was not a whit smarter   once he swallowed the words.

Riddle 49

Ic wat eardfæstne   anne standan,
deafne, dumban,   se oft dæges swilgeð
þurh gopes hond   gifrum lacum.
Hwilum on þam wicum   se wonna þegn,
sweart ond saloneb,   sendeð oþre
under goman him   golde dyrran,
þa æþelingas   oft wilniað,
cyningas ond cwene.   Ic þæt cyn nu gen
nemnan ne wille,   þe him to nytte swa
ond to dugþum doþ   þæt se dumba her,
eorp unwita,   ær forswilgeð.

     I know someone who stands,   stuck fast in the earth.
     He's deaf and dumb,   and by day he gulps down
     the finest burnt offerings,   hand-fed by a slave.
     Sometimes in his dwelling,   a dingy servant,
     swarthy and sallow-faced,   sends other things
     down his gullet   which are dearer than gold,
     and which athelings   often crave,
     even kings and queens.   Yet his kin's name
     I will not utter—   for the use and help
     of men, they make   what this mute one,
     sooty and stupid,   swallows up first.

Riddle 50

Wiga is on eorþan   wundrum acenned
dryhtum to nytte,   of dumbum twam
torht atyhted,   þone on teon wigeð
feond his feonde.   Forstrangne oft
wif hine wrið;   he him wel hereð,
þeowaþ him geþwære,   gif him þegniað
mægeð ond mæcgas   mid gemete ryhte,
fedað hine fægre;   he him fremum stepeð
life on lissum.   Leanað grimme
þam þe hine wloncne   weorþan læteð.

    There's a warrior on earth,   wondrously begotten
for lords' benefit,   brought forth in splendor
by two dumb fellows.   A foeman brings him
to destroy his foe—   but, strong as he is,
a woman often binds him.   He obeys them well,
serves them in peace,   if sons and daughters
feed and foster   the fair-looking one
in proper measure;   he multiplies comfort
for gladness in life.   He grimly repays
the one who lets him   grow lofty and haughty.

Riddle 51

*Ic seah wrætlice wuhte feower
samed siþian; swearte wæran lastas,
swaþu swiþe blacu. Swift wæs on fore,
fuglum framra; fleag on lyfte,
deaf under yþe. Dreag unstille
winnende wiga se him wegas tæcneþ
ofer fæted gold feower eallum.*

    I once witnessed   four wondrous beings
travelling together.   Their trails were dusky,
their footsteps black.   The fastest led them;
more swiftly than birds   he soared aloft
and dove under wave.   A doughty warrior
persevered in pointing   the path to all four,
so that they might ride   over richest gold.

Riddle 52

Ic seah ræpingas   in ræced fergan
under hrof sales   hearde twegen,
þa wæron genamnan,   nearwum bendum
gefeterade   fæste togædre;
þara oþrum wæs   an getenge
wonfah Wale,   seo weold hyra
bega siþe   bendum fæstra.

    I saw captives   carried into the house,
    beneath the hall roof—   a hardened pair,
    they had been taken   and tied together,
    fettered firmly,   held fast in bondage.
    One was pressed hard   by a Welsh slave;
    the dusky woman   drove them both
    along on their journey,   joined by their fetters.

Riddle 54

Hyse cwom gangan, þær he hie wisse
stondan in wincsele, stop feorran to,
hror hægstealdmon, hof his agen
hrægl hondum up, hrand under gyrdels
hyre stondendre stiþes nathwæt,
worhte his willan; wagedan buta.
Þegn onnette, wæs þragum nyt
tillic esne, teorode hwæþre
æt stunda gehwam strong ær þon hio,
werig þæs weorces. Hyre weaxan ongon
under gyrdelse þæt oft gode men
ferðþum freogað ond mid feo bicgað.

    So this guy walks in, goes over to the corner
    where he knew she'd be standing. This stout fellow
    (who hailed from afar) hitched his own clothes
    up with his hands, and under her girdle
    he stuck a stiff thingie, as she was standing right there.
    He worked his will as they wiggled and shook.
    Our hero hurried— he had his uses!
    Still, this strong and steadfast servant
    grew weary of the work, wore out every time
    sooner than *she* did. Then something began
    to grow under her girdle which good men often
    prize in their minds and pay for dearly.

Riddle 57

*Ðeos lyft byreð lytle wihte
ofer beorghleoþa. Þa sind blace swiþe,
swearte salopade. Sanges rope
heapum feað, hlude cirmað,
tredað bearonæssas, hwilum burgsalo
niþþa bearna. Nemnað hy sylfe.*

    The breezes loft   these little creatures
    over craggy peaks.   Their coats are quite black,
    swarthy and sooty.   Singing freely,
    they crowd together,   clamoring loudly,
    at home in forests   or in fortresses built
    by the sons of men.   They speak their own names.

Riddle 60

Ic wæs be sonde,   sæwealle neah,
æt merefarope,   minum gewunade
frumstapole fæst;   fea ænig wæs
monna cynnes,   þæt minne þær
on anæde   eard beheolde,
ac mec uhtna gehwam   yð sio brune
lagufæðme beleolc.   Lyt ic wende
þæt ic ær oþþe sið   æfre sceolde
ofer meodubence   muðleas sprecan,
wordum wrixlan.   Þæt is wundres dæl,
on sefan searolic   þam þe swylc ne conn,
hu mec seaxes ord   ond seo swiþre hond,
eorles ingeþonc   ond ord somod,
þingum geþydan,   þæt ic wiþ þe sceolde
for unc anum twam   ærendspræce
abeodan bealdlice,   swa hit beorna ma
uncre wordcwidas   widdor ne mænden.

Beside the sound,   by sea-cliffs, I lived
where whitecaps crashed,   clinging fast
to my first home.   Few were those
of the kindred of men   who came to see
that wild wasteland   where I was born,
but each day before dawn   the dusky wave
dandled me in its lap.   Little did I think
that someday I   should ever speak
(though missing a mouth)   at the mead-bench,
weaving words.   A wondrous thing,
a clever trick to those   who cannot do it:
how a knife's steel tip,   a strong right hand,
and a man's mind   all merge together
in such a way   that I can speak with you,
boldly proclaiming   a private message
for us two only.   No others can spread
our words more widely;   we alone know them.

Riddle 61

Oft mec fæste bileac freolicu meowle,
ides on earce, hwilum up ateah
folmum sinum ond frean sealde,
holdum þeodne, swa hio haten wæs.
Siðþan me on hreþre heafod sticade,
nioþan upweardne, on nearo fegde.
Gif þæs ondfengan ellen dohte,
mec frætwedne fyllan sceolde
ruwes nathwæt. Ræd hwæt ic mæne.

    A lovely lady often locked me up
    tight in her treasure-box— but took me out sometimes,
    with her own fingers offered me to her lord,
    the brave ruler, as he bade her do.
    Then he stuck his head straight into my middle,
    up from beneath: a narrow squeeze!
    If the valiant prince had vigor enough,
    I had to be filled— though finely adorned—
    with some rough thing. Now reckon my meaning.

Riddle 64

Ic seah ᚹ ond ᛁ ofer wong faran,
beran ᛒ ᛗ; bæm wæs on siþþe
hæbbendes hyht ᚻ ond ᚠ
swylce þryþa dæl, ᚦ ond ᛗ.
Gefeah ᚠ ond ᚱ fleah ofer ᛠ
ᚻ ond ᛈ sylfes þæs folces.

   I saw H and O heading over the field,
   bearing M and A. Both on their way
   were happy to have an H and A,
   such a thewful troop of T and H.
   And F and A exulting flew over the S:
   the S and P of the people themselves.

Riddle 65

Cwico wæs ic ne cwæð ic wiht   cwele ic efne sepeah
ær ic wæs eft ic cwom   æghwa mec reafað
hafað mec on headre   ond min heafod scireþ
biteð mec on bær lic   briceð mine wisan
monnan ic ne bite   nymþþe he me bite
sindan þara monige   þe mec bitað.

       Saying nothing, I lived;   even so, I die.
       I once was; I returned.   Everyone takes me,
       keeps me confined,   cuts into my head,
       bites my bare body   and breaks my stem.
       I don't bite a man   unless he bites me;
       indeed there are many   who do bite me.

Riddle 66

Ic eom mare   þonne þes middangeard,
læsse þonne hondwyrm,   leohtre þonne mona,
swiftre þonne sunne.   Sæs me sind ealle
flodas on fæðmum   ond þes foldan bearm,
grene wongas.   Grundum ic hrine,
helle underhnige,   heofonas oferstige,
wuldres eþel,   wide ræce
ofer engla eard,   eorþan gefylle,
ealne middangeard   ond merestreamas
side mid me sylfum.   Saga hwæt ic hatte.

    I am mightier   than Midgard's self,
    yet smaller than a bug—   brighter than moon,
    swifter than sun.   Seas and floods
    are all in my embrace,   the earth's bosom
    and the green meadows.   I move through the depths,
    sink beneath hell   and soar above the heavens,
    the realms of splendor.   I range widely,
    over the angels' estate;   amply I fill
    the earth and all Midgard   and mighty seas
    with my own self.   Say what I'm called.

Riddle 68, 69

Ic þa wiht geseah   on weg feran
heo wæs wrætlice   wundrum gegierwed.

Wundor wearð on wege   wæter wearð to bane.

    I saw this creature   start out on a journey,
    dearly adorned,   decked out with wonders.

    A wonder on waves: water became bone.

Riddle 70

Wiht is wrætlic   þam þe hyre wisan ne conn.
Singeð þurh sidan.   Is se sweora woh,
orþoncum geworht;   hafaþ eaxle tua
scearp on gescyldrum.   His gesceapo dreogeð
þe swa wrætlice   be wege stonde
heah ond hleortorht   hæleþum to nytte.

    A curious creature,   if you can't compass her ways—
    she sings through her sides.   Her skillfully worked
    neck is crooked;   she carries two pointed
    shoulders on her back.   She suffers her fate
    when in her splendor   she stands by the road,
    bright-faced and tall   for the benefit of men.

Riddle 74

Ic wæs fæmne geong, feaxhar cwene,
ond ænlic rinc on ane tid;
fleah mid fuglum ond on flode swom,
deaf under ype dead mid fiscum,
ond on foldan stop, hæfde ferð cwicu.

    I was a young girl, a grey-haired lady,
    an excellent man. All at the same time
    I soared with birds and swam in the ocean;
    dead, I dived with fishes under drifting waves,
    and alighted on land; I held living souls.

Riddle 77

Sæ mec fedde,   sundhelm þeahte,
ond mec yþa wrugon   eorþan getenge
feþelease.   Oft ic flode ongean
muð ontynde.   Nu wile monna sum
min flæsc fretan,   felles ne recceð,
siþþan he me of sidan   seaxes orde
hyd arypeð,   ...ec hr... ...þe siþþan
iteð unsodene   ea... ....d.

        The sea fed me,   salt-foam sheltered me,
        waves enwrapped me,   weighted me to earth
        where I stood footless,   facing the current,
        often gaping my mouth.   A man now wishes
        to feast on my flesh,   not feeling for my doom,
        as he raises his knife-point   and rips my hide
        off from my sides,   then swallows me ra—

Riddle 79, 80

Ic eom æþelinges   æht on willa.
Ic eom æþelinges   eaxlgestealla,
fyrdrinces gefara,   frean minum leof,
cyninges geselda.   Cwen mec hwilum
hwitloccedu   hond on legeð,
eorles dohtor,   þeah hio æþelu sy.
Hæbbe me on bosme   þæt on bearwe geweox.
Hwilum ic on wloncum   wicge ride
herges on ende;   heard is min tunge.
Oft ic woðboran   wordleana sum
agyfe æfter giedde.   Good is min wise
ond ic sylfa salo.   Saga hwæt ic hatte.

    I am the warrior's   will and power.
    I am the warrior's   warmest friend,
    a champion's companion,   cherished by my lord,
    comrade of a king.   Even a queen, sometimes,
    with light locks of hair,   lays her hands on me,
    though the lady be royal,   a ruler's daughter.
    What grew in the grove   I guard in my breast.
    On a spirited steed   I sometimes ride
    at the head of the host;   harsh is my voice.
    I often pay a poet   the prize that's his due,
    reward for his words.   My ways are good;
    I myself am swarthy.   Say what I'm called.

Riddle 85

Nis min sele swige,   ne ic sylfa hlud
ymb ...   unc dryhten scop
siþ ætsomne.   Ic eom swiftre þonne he,
þragum strengra,   he þreohtigra.
Hwilum ic me reste;   he sceal yrnan forð.
Ic him in wunige   a þenden ic lifge;
gif wit unc gedælað,   me bið dead witod.

    My home is not silent   nor am I myself loud;
    it's the Lord's plan   that the pair of us
    should fare together.   I am faster than he,
    sometimes hardier.   He holds out longer.
    I rest now and then;   he must run onwards.
    As long as I live,   I'll lodge with him;
    if we two separate,   it's certain death for me.

Riddle 86

Wiht cwom gongan   þær weras sæton
monige on mæðle,   mode snottre;
hæfde an eage   ond earan twa,
ond II fet,   XII hund heafda,
hrycg ond wombe   ond honda twa,
earmas ond eaxle,   anne sweoran
ond sidan twa.   Saga hwæt ic hatte.

> A creature came into   a council of men,
> where many sages   were seated together.
> It had one eye;   its ears were two,
> with two feet also,   twelve hundred heads,
> two hands, a back   and a belly as well,
> arms and shoulders,   a single neck
> and two sides.   Say what I'm called.

Riddle 91

Min heafod is   homere geþuren,
searopila wund,   sworfen feole.
Oft ic begine   þæt me ongean sticað,
þonne ic hnitan sceal,   hringum gyrded,
hearde wið heardum,   hindan þyrel,
forð ascufan   þæt mines frean
mod Ϸ freoþað   middelnihtum.
Hwilum ic under bæc   bregde nebbe,
hyrde þæs hordes,   þonne min hlaford wile
lafe þicgan   þara þe he of life het
wælcræfte awrecan   willum sinum.

> My head is pounded   by hammer blows,
> stabbed by points,   scoured with a file.
> I often clench in my mouth   what clashes against me
> when, bound with rings,   I must batter against
> a hole from behind,   hardness against hardness,
> pressing forth, so that   my prince may keep
> his mind at ease   in the middle of the night.
> Treasure-keeper, at times   I twist my beak
> backwards, when my lord   collects the goods
> of men whom he'd sworn   to slay at his will,
> to drive from life   by his deadly power.

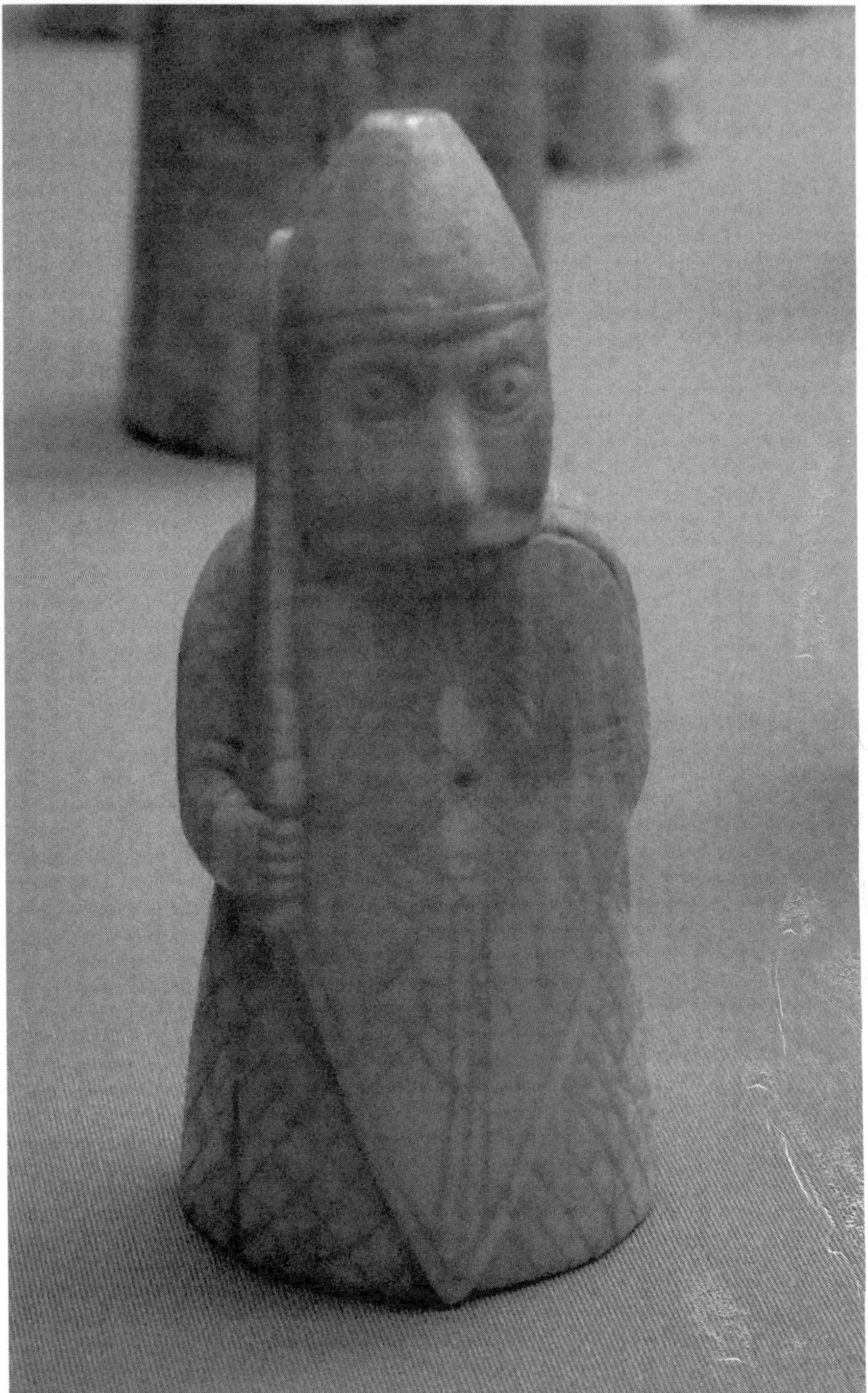

Riddle 1, *Solomon and Saturn*

Saturnus cuæð:
"Ac hwæt is se dumba,   se ðe on sumre dene resteð?
Swiðe snyttrað,   hafað seofon tungan;
hafað tungena gehwylc   XX orda,
hafað orda gehwylc   engles snytro,
ðara ðe wile anra hwylc   uppe bringan,
ðæt ðu ðære gyldnan gesiehst   Hierusalem
weallas blican   and hiera winrod lixan,
soðfæstra segn.   Saga hwæt ic mæne."

Salomon cuæð:
"Bec sindon breme,   bodiað geneahhe
weotodne willan   ðam ðe wiht hygeð.
Gestrangað hie and gestaðeliað   staðolfæstne geðoht,
amyrgað modsefan   manna gehwylces
of ðreamedlan   ðisses lifes."

Saturn said:
What dumb one dwells   down in a certain valley?
He is swift to enlighten;   he has seven tongues.
each of his tongues   bears twenty points;
each and every point   has an angel's wisdom,
each one wishes   to exalt you on high,
that you may glimpse   golden Jerusalem,
the brilliant walls   and the bright cross of joy,
the sign of the righteous.   Say what I mean.

Solomon said:
Books are renowned,   abundantly proclaiming
true purpose to him   who ponders them a bit.
They support and strengthen   steadfast thought;
they ease the mind   of every man
from sorrows and cares   suffered in this life.

Riddle 2 from *Solomon and Saturn*

Saturnus cwæð:
"Ac hwæt is ðæt wundor   ðe geond ðas worold færeð,
styrnenga gæð,   staðolas beateð,
aweceð wopdropan,   winneð oft hider?
Ne mæg hit steorra ne stan   ne se steapa gimm,
wæter ne wildeor   wihte beswican,
ac him on hand gæð   heardes and hnesces,
micles and mætes;   him to mose sceall
gegangan geara gehwelce   grundbuendra,
lyftfleogendra,   laguswemmendra,
ðria ðreoteno   ðusendgerimes."

Salomon cwæð:
"Yldo beoð on eorðan   æghwæs cræftig;
mid hiðendre   hildewræsne,
rumre racenteage,   ræceð wide,
langre linan,   lisseð eall ðæt heo wile.
Beam heo abreoteð   and bebriceð telgum,
astyreð standendne   stefn on siðe,
afilleð hine on foldan;   friteð æfter ðam
wildne fugol.   Heo oferwigeð wulf,
hio oferbideð stanas,   heo oferstigeð style,
hio abiteð iren mid ome,   deð usic swa."

Saturn said:
But what wonder is that,   wending across the land
on its baleful march?   It batters down columns,
awakens weeping,   makes war on us often.
Neither star nor stone   nor stately gem,
not water nor wild beast   can outwit it one bit;
into its hands come   the hard and the soft,
the large and the small.   All land-dwelling beasts,
and those that soar in the sky   or that swim in the waters
must enter its clutches   and be utterly devoured:
three times thirteen   thousands, all told.

Solomon said:
Old age has power   over all in the world.
With chains that seek out   slaves to capture,
spacious shackles,   long snare lines,
she grasps far and wide,   gathers all she wants.
She smashes down the tree   and snaps off twigs,
shakes up the standing   stock in the end
and fells it to the ground,   then feeds afterwards
on the wild bird.   She outwars the wolf,
she outlives the stone,   she outlasts steel,
gnaws iron with rust—   to us she is no different.

ANSWERS

Riddle 1: A thunderstorm on land, whose lightning starts fires, and whose "cover" is the clouds. Riddles 1-3 all deal with storms of some sort, and are sometimes considered to form a single riddle, or else Riddles 2 and 3 are considered to make up one riddle. I believe that all three work best as self-contained riddles, but there are evident thematic links between them.

Riddle 2: A storm at sea. Today we might answer this riddle as "active geological fault"—that being something under the waves that is very much capable of stirring them up to destruction. The imagery of a leader who controls the storm may have been understood by Christians as a reference to Jesus's ability to calm storms. But several expressions resonate with pre-Christian myth—*garsecg*, literally "spear-man," and *gifen*, possibly related to the name of the Norse goddess Gefjon, both are used for "sea". The mention of pulling the speaker up from the depths reminds me of the Midgard Serpent being fished up by Thor.

Riddle 5: A shield.

Riddle 7: A swan.

Riddle 8: A nightingale.

Riddle 11: A silver cup of strong drink.

Riddle 13: Ten chicks. The "skin garments" are the membranes inside their abandoned eggshells; the "new garb" is the feathers they will grow.

Riddle 14: A horn. Some lines seemingly refer to a blowing-horn, and others to a drinking-horn. See Riddle 80.

Riddle 16: An anchor.

Riddle 17: Many scholars solve this riddle as "chest for weapons", "catapult", "quiver of arrows", or "ballista" (a giant crossbow-like siege weapon). Marijane Osborn has proposed a clever solution that I think is more likely to be right: "beehive"—specifically a skep, a straw beehive made like an upside-down basket.[3]

Riddle 19: The four groups of Anglo-Saxon runes in the original riddle, spelled backwards, read HORS (horse), MON (man), WEGA (ways), and HAOFOC (hawk). I've translated and in some cases slightly modified the names of the rune letters, and altered the words that they spell out to Modern English.

Riddle 21: A plough.

Riddle 22: Polar constellations. The wagon is Ursa Major or the Big Dipper, which is referred to in Old English and later sources as the Wain or Wagon. The "pole" could either be the north celestial pole, marked by the star Polaris, or the star Arcturus, known in folklore as the "Wagon-Pole" marking an extension of the harness of the Wagon. The apparent rotation of the heavens makes the Wagon appear to cross the sky without touching the horizon, as seen from mid-northern latitudes; thus the Wagon never touches or sinks below sea or land. The sixty horsemen with eleven stallions snd four bright horses that ride on the Wagon are also circumpolar stars, although scholars have debated exactly which stars are intended.[4]

Riddle 23: A bow. The text starts with the word *agob*, which spelled backwards is *boga*, "bow" in Old English.

Riddle 24: The runes in the original manuscript have the names "gift", "ash-tree", "riding", "one of the Æsir-gods", "hail" and "ice". They spell out **gærohi**—which is meaningless, but which can be rearranged into the answer to this riddle: **higoræ**. By modifying (and in one case completely replacing) the rune names in my translation, I came up with six words whose first letters spell out **pagemi**. Rearrange those letters to spell the answer in modern English: a **magpie**.

Riddle 27: Mead. Anyone who doubts the part about "dealing blows to blockheads in broad daylight" has never had a mead hangover. . .

Riddle 28: Barley, brewed into ale. Translating this riddle leaves a lot of leeway for interpretation. The rhyming lines aren't specific enough to know exactly what is meant here, but it seems at least plausible that they refer to the process of harvesting, malting, and roasting grain. "After its death" may refer to the metaphorical death of the harvested grain and its resurrection as ale—think of "John Barleycorn" here. Some scholars solve it as "harp" or other musical instrument made of wood. But the previous riddle is pretty obviously "mead", and I rather like the idea that these two riddles go together.

Riddle 29: The crescent moon, obscured by the rising sun; the "plunder" is the moon's light. A waning crescent moon in the morning sky will seem to disappear for a few days until it reappears as a waxing crescent in the evening sky; this may be why no one knows where the moon has gone.

Riddle 31: A bagpipe. The creature's "neck" would be the blowpipe; the "foot" is the chanter; the "brothers on her neck" are the drones. Her "hoard" might be the air filling the bag.

Riddle 32: A ship.

Riddle 33: An iceberg. Her mother and daughter, of course, are both liquid water.

Riddle 34: A rake.

Riddle 35: Chainmail. This riddle is noteworthy for several reasons: it's a translation of one of Aldhelm's Latin riddles, and it also exists in a version written in the Northumbrian dialect, known as the *Leiden Riddle* for the city where the manuscript is kept. There's also a pun at the end: *searu* can mean "craftiness, cleverness" and "armor", so the word *searoponcum* means both "with crafty thoughts" and "with thoughts about armor." My translation "if your wits are on guard" is an imperfect attempt to convey the pun.

Riddle 36: This may be a blend of two riddles; it is unusual for a riddle to ask for its solution twice. The first six lines have been solved as "two pregnant women riding a pregnant horse"—or the wings could be accommodated as "a man with a hawk and his pregnant wife riding a pregnant horse". However, I think the best solution to the entire riddle is a ship—the four "feet" below the belly are four oars, the eight on its back are the feet of the four oarsmen, and the six heads and twelve eyes belong to the oarsmen and two figureheads. The forms of a horse, hound, bird, and woman refer to figureheads or other carvings on the ship; more likely, the "horse" may be a metaphor for the ship itself, and the "bird" would be the winglike sail, leaving the hound and woman to be the two figureheads.

I have left out a line added between the half-lines of line 4, probably a marginal note that was incorporated by an unskillful copyist. It reads

monn *h w M* wiif *m x l kf wf* hors *qxxs*

This is a common medieval cipher in which each vowel is replaced by the following consonant in the alphabet. The line includes scribal mistakes, such as replacing the letter *p* with the letter *wynn* for *w* (which looks much like a *p*). With the errors fixed, the line reads

monn *homo*   wif *mulier*   hors *equus*

These are the words for "man", "woman", and "horse", respectively. This may be a guess at the answer. It could also just be a note left by someone who did not know English well (or Latin well), as all three words are used in the riddle.

Riddle 37: A bellows.

Riddle 38: A male calf nursing on milk. The "four springs" are the mother cow's teats; "Binding the living" presumably refers to using leather thongs to tie someone up. There's a pun in the original that I couldn't figure out how to translate; *on gesceap* is usually interpreted as "to his delight", but it could also mean "in the genitals", possibly referring to the location of the udder. *Wæpnedcynnes* also has a double meaning; it can mean "of the weaponed kind", "of the sort that carries weapons", and could refer to the horns of the young bull (as *wæpen* does in Riddle 14). But *wæpned* was so commonly used to specify men—because free men were obliged to carry weapons—that it came to mean just "male", and *wæpnedcynnes* can also mean "of the male sex."

Riddle 39: This is one of the most mysterious riddles in the Exeter Book. Various scholars have proposed "Day", "Cloud", "Moon", "Time", and "Dream". But the solution that I think fits the riddle best is "Death"—it comes only once to every living thing; it cannot affect those who are either immortal in Heaven, or already dead in Hell; it wields great power, despite not having a body or mind; and it can bring comfort.[5]

Riddle 44: A key.

Riddle 45: Rising bread dough.

Riddle 47: A book-boring insect.

Riddle 49: A baker and his oven.

Riddle 50: Fire. The two "dumb fellows" are the two sticks that give birth to the fire through friction, or else the flint and steel used to strike sparks.

Riddle 51: The "four wondrous beings" are three fingers holding a quill pen, which "soars" and "dives" when it is lifted and dipped in an inkwell. The gold that they ride over is presumably the gold of an illuminated manuscript. All four are directed by a "warrior", the scribe (or at least the scribe's arm). Several riddles by Aldhelm, Tatwine, and Eusebius use similar motifs, such as the "dark tracks", but this riddle is not directly based on any of them.[6]

Riddle 52: Probably a flail—an agricultural implement made of two wooden beams chained together. Others have argued for a pair of buckets, either carried by a cord over the shoulders, or dipped alternately into a well. The word *Wale* or *Weale*, the feminine of *Wealh*, originally meant simply "foreigner", but in Anglo-Saxon England specifically meant one of the Celtic-speaking peoples in the west, i.e. a Welsh person. Since there was a custom of capturing the Welsh as slaves, *Wealh/Weale* came to mean "slave" as well.

Riddle 54: A man making butter in a churn.

Riddle 57: Swallows. These birds make a wide variety of warbling calls, some of which could conceivably have sounded to Old English speakers like their name *swealwe*.

Riddle 60: Some have proposed that the answer is "a pen made from a reed." But the poem that comes right after this one in the *Exeter Book* is "The Husband's Message", in which a man sends a message carved in runes to his wife. Many scholars have suggested that this is intentional, and that this riddle refers to a rune-stick—perhaps one made of driftwood. Some have argued that Riddle 60 and "The Husband's Message" should be considered two parts of the same poem.[7]

Riddle 61: A helmet, or possibly a shirt.

Riddle 64: Each pair of runes is the beginning of a word. ᚹ ᛁ stands for *wicg*, "horse", ᛒ ᛗ is *beorn*, "man", and ᚾ ᚠ is *hafoc*, "hawk". ᚦ ᛗ is either *þegnas*, "thanes", or *þeōwas*, "servants"; ᚠ ᚱ is probably *falcen*, "falcon"; ᛏ is *ēar*, "ground" (or possibly *ear*, "ocean"); and ᚻ ᛚ is *spere*, "spear." So the whole riddle describes a scene of a lord— kenned as *folces spere*, the "spear [defender] of the people"—and his thanes or his servants, riding out and hunting with hawks.

Riddle 65: An onion. The line "I once was; I returned" might refer to the habit of some onion varieties of producing extra bulbs or cloves, meaning that most of an onion could be eaten while a small part could be saved for planting later.

Riddle 66: The scholars say that the "right answer" is Creation—i.e. the entire universe. This is probably what the riddle's author meant. But I like the answer of the twelve-year-old daughter of scholar Louise Bragg, who suggested that the answer is Imagination.[8]

Riddle 68, 69: It's not clear if we have one riddle or two; these are considered separate riddles by Krapp and Dobie. The first two lines are almost identical with the first two lines of Riddle 36, but by themselves are not enough to make a guessable riddle. The last line is complete in itself, and the answer is ice.

Riddle 70: A musical pipe cut from a reed, or possibly from an elder or willow tree, which have easily hollowed-out branches. The lines about how "she stands by the road" refer to the reed or tree branch, before it is harvested and cut into shape.

Riddle 74: Jennifer Culver[9] has suggested that the answer is a valkyrie (Old English *wælcyrige*), a female messenger of the god Woden who could travel anywhere. However, I have followed John D. Niles's suggestion that the answer is a ship—which is transformed from a young sapling to a grey mature tree to a completed ship, which in a storm may indeed be tossed into the air and plunge under waves, yet in the end be drawn up on land by the living men it has carried.[10]

Riddle 77: An oyster. The text is damaged right at the point where the oyster describes itself being eaten, which I think creates a nicely macabre effect, even though the poet could not have intended it.

Riddle 79, 80: A horn. In both this riddle and Riddle 14, some lines seemingly refer to a blowing-horn, and others to a drinking-horn. Krapp and Dobie considered the line *Ic eom æpelinges æht on willa* as a separate riddle, although there's no way to guess the answer, and the manuscript appears to separate the line as a separate riddle. In this case I have followed Williamson, who argues that they should be considered one riddle.

Riddle 85: A fish in a stream.

Riddle 86: A one-eyed man who sells garlic. (We only know the answer because this riddle is based on a Latin riddle by Symphosius, which states the answer explicitly.) This is a fine example of a "neck-riddle"—a riddle that cannot realistically be answered by logical deduction from the clues given. Neck riddles are so called because a folktale hero may use a "neck riddle" to save his neck and outwit his opponent in a contest. Examples include Bilbo Baggins's "What have I got in my pocket?" in *The Hobbit*, and Odin's "What did Odin whisper in his son's ear as he lay on the pyre?" in the Eddic poem *Vafþrúðnismál* and the saga *Hervarar saga ok Heiðreks*.

Riddle 91: A key. Unlike Riddle 44, this is not a double entendre. The manuscript uses the rune letter ᚹ as an abbreviation; the rune's name is *wynn*, "joy; happiness".

Riddle 1, *Solomon and Saturn*: The "dumb one" in a valley is a book on its shelf. Its "seven tongues" are the seven vowels of the Old English language, and the "twenty points" are the twenty consonants, which of course cannot be sounded without adding one of the "tongues" to make up a syllable.

Riddle 2, *Solomon and Saturn*: This riddle is probably the inspiration for one of Tolkien's riddles in *The Hobbit*—the one that begins "This thing all things devours, / Birds, beasts, trees, flowers. . . ."

NOTES

1. George Philip Krapp and Elliott Van Kirk Dobie, *The Exeter Book. Anglo-Saxon Poetic Records*, Vol. III. New York: Columbia University Press, 1936. p. ix.

2. Craig Williamson, *The Old English Riddles of the Exeter Book*. Chapel Hill, N.C.: University of North Carolina Press, 1977. pp. 3-12.

3. Osborne, Marijane. "'Skep' (*Beinenkorb, *beoleap*) As A Culture-Specific Solution To Exeter Book Riddle 17." *ANQ*, vol. 18, no. 1 (2005), pp. 7-18.

4. Patrick J. Murphy, *Unriddling the Exeter Riddles*, Penn State University Press, 2011. Pp. 111-123. See also Williamson, pp. 201-204.

5. Erika von Erhardt-Siebold. "Old English Riddle No. 39: Creature Death". *PMLA*, vol. 61, no. 4 (1946), pp. 910-915.

6. Williamson, pp. 293-295.

7. James E. Anderson. *Two Literary Riddles in the Exeter Book*. Norman, Okla., University of Oklahoma Press, 1986. Pp. 144-150.

8. Bragg, Louise. *The Lyric Speakers of Old English Poetry*, Fairleigh Dickinson University Press, 1991. Pp. 47-48.

9. Culver, Jennifer. *Bridging the Gap: Finding a Valkyrie in a Riddle*. M.A. Thesis, University of North Texas, 2007. 76 pp.

10. Niles, John D. "Exeter Book Riddle 74 and the Play of the Text." *Anglo-Saxon England*, vol. 29 (1998), pp. 169-207.

Made in the USA
San Bernardino, CA
02 January 2018